Writing Experiences for Young Learners

by Marilee Woodfield
illustrated by Janet Armbrust

Publisher
Key Education Publishing Company, LLC
Minneapolis, Minnesota

CONGRATULATIONS ON YOUR PURCHASE OF A KEY EDUCATION PRODUCT!

The editors at Key Education are former teachers who bring experience, enthusiasm, and quality to each and every product. Thousands of teachers have looked to the staff at Key Education for new and innovative resources to make their work more enjoyable and rewarding. We are committed to developing educational materials that will assist teachers in building a strong and developmentally appropriate curriculum for young children.

PLAN FOR GREAT TEACHING EXPERIENCES WHEN YOU USE EDUCATIONAL MATERIALS FROM KEY EDUCATION PUBLISHING COMPANY, LLC

Credits

Author: Marilee Woodfield
Publisher: Sherrill B. Flora
Editors: Debra Pressnall and Kelly Morris Huxmann
Inside Illustrations: Janet Armbrust
Page Design and Layout: Debra Pressnall
Cover Design: Annette Hollister-Papp
Children's Stories on Cover: Will and Kassie
Cover Photo Credit: © Shutterstock

Key Education welcomes manuscripts and product ideas from teachers. For a copy of our submission guidelines, please send a self-addressed stamped envelope to:
Key Education Publishing Company, LLC
Acquisitions Department
9601 Newton Avenue South
Minneapolis, Minnesota 55431

About the Author

Marilee Woodfield graduated with a bachelor of science in human development from Brigham Young University. In addition to teaching and directing preschools for 20 years, she has written more than 15 resource books for early childhood educators. Marilee also spends her time driving the family taxi service and completing various home-improvement projects. She currently resides in Texas with her husband and four children.

Copyright Notice

Standard Book Number: 978-1-933052-72-4
Writing Experiences for Young Learners
Copyright © 2007 by Key Education Publishing Company, LLC
Minneapolis, Minnesota 55431

Table of Contents

# Introduction

Most parents and educators can tell you that a firm grasp on literacy skills equals success in school and beyond. The importance of reading has been well documented; however, other components of literacy, such as writing and storytelling, have garnered far less attention. *Writing Experiences for Young Learners* helps to fill in this gap. Providing activities for emergent and beginning writers, as well as useful information for educators, this book:

- **Defines standards and skills** — Learn what is developmentally appropriate writing, and what the standards are for teaching each age and stage.

- **Explains emergent writing** — See the importance of writing in connection with other literacy skills, and how parents can support the process of learning how to write.

- **Highlights writing basics** — Gather tips for strengthening the mechanics and content of children's writing.

- **Creates a writing environment** — Give children the tools to compose in various ways.

- **Facilitates writing activities** — Offer a variety of writing activities that target the development of beginning to more advanced writing skills.

The lessons presented in this resource cover a range of skills. Beginning writing experiences that include simple ideas for alternative pencil/paper activities and writing words. More advanced lessons address topics such as writing complete sentences, sequencing (finding the beginning, middle, and end of a story), and interviewing to find out information.

Each activity in *Writing Experiences for Young Learners* is broad enough to correlate with multiple curriculum themes, if desired, or works well as a stand-alone activity for writing experiences. Suggestions for expanding or simplifying the activity ideas are also included to help you adapt each idea to a broad range of abilities. Additionally, cross-curricular activities and suggestions have been provided to show the natural integration of writing experiences into other areas of the curriculum.

Learning to write is a process. Preschoolers can strengthen their fine-motor skills with simple activities, such as stringing beads, working with molding dough, cutting paper, drawing pictures, painting scenes, and so on. Kindergartners can be introduced to very basic punctuation, the conventional spellings of a few simple words, spacing between words, letter-sound connections, and simplified story organization. First graders will be ready for more advanced writing skills, such as the conventional spellings of words, correct punctuation of sentences, and independent writing.

Young children can and should learn that writing is a way of communicating thoughts and information, and that writing can be found everywhere. Giving children opportunities to interact with writing in a variety of ways will help foster the development of their writing skills. As you use the activity ideas presented in this book, make sure that you adapt them appropriately for the children. This will help children develop an interest in writing without feeling overwhelmed. Before you know it, you may be surrounded by a whole classroom of great (and eager) writers!

# Developmental Writing

When it comes to teaching children about writing, research has shown that more is better. The more often children are exposed to rich oral language and print experiences, and the more they are given opportunities to compose, the better writers they will become.

Keep in mind that these writing experiences should be appropriate for the age and stage of development of each child. Requiring children to write beyond their developmental capacity does not push them to be better writers. Instead, it may cause those children to become frustrated and avoid writing altogether. It is important to remember that skill development happens on a continuum and is different for each child. While some preschoolers may be able to write their first and last names with ease, other children may not be proficient at this skill until they reach kindergarten. The key is to provide writing opportunities that allow children to write at their own levels—whatever those may be.

Writing success comes when writing is relevant and enjoyable. Choose meaningful topics, such as personal experiences. Have the children write about things they are doing or learning in class. Be sure to include opportunities to write when working on other curricular activities, too, such as recording scientific discoveries. And, above all, remember to express encouragement for the children's efforts, not just their successes.

The development of writing skills follows a predictable path:

- At first, the child scribbles exclusively.

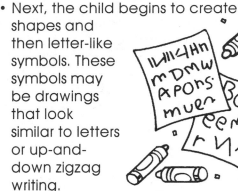

- Next, the child begins to create shapes and then letter-like symbols. These symbols may be drawings that look similar to letters or up-and-down zigzag writing.

During this stage, children may also start to recognize and copy important words, phrases, and simple sentences, such as their names and the words *Mommy*, *Daddy*, and *I love you*.

- Zigzag writing is now replaced with "words." Those words that the child does not know how to spell will be created phonetically (using invented spelling).

- Finally, the child begins to generate ideas independently and starts to write legibly, using conventional spelling and punctuation.

Writing Standards

If the amount of time we focus on a subject is indicative of its importance, then it is not difficult to understand the focus of literacy skills. When we speak of literacy, our thoughts generally turn first to reading skills and rightly so, because reading is a key component of literacy. However, writing is also an important aspect of literacy, and it is intertwined with reading in a complex web of skills.

Learning that speech can be written down, that print conveys messages, that letters make words, and that words make sentences are all ways that children learn how print and spoken words are related. This process of learning to write and read is a challenging and magical time. As children progress through these skills, it is important to foster their independence. This will result in some spelling and grammatical missteps along the way. You may find the letters to parents on page 7 helpful in explaining this process to families.

The following list of standards offers a guideline of what to expect at each stage of a child's development:

Preschooler

- Begins to recognize that print conveys a message
- Begins to understand the conventions of print (i.e., text flows from left to right; letters make words; words make sentences)
- Scribbles and uses shapes or letter-like symbols for letters
- Experiments with a growing variety of writing tools and materials
- Writes his or her own name and other important words (*Mommy*, *Daddy*, etc.)
- Writes the alphabet in uppercase letters
- Dictates messages and stories for others to write

Kindergartner

- Writes his or her own name and other important words
- Writes both uppercase and lowercase letters of the alphabet
- Uses invented spellings or phonetic spellings to create words
- Understands that print conveys a message
- Understands the conventions of print (i.e., text flows from left to right and from top to bottom on a page; letters make words; words make sentences)
- Has increasing control of penmanship, uses spaces between words, and makes letters similar in size
- Retells a story as heard and can generate ideas for stories

First Grader

- Writes each uppercase and lowercase letter of the alphabet using correct formation and adequate spacing
- Uses text and illustrations to express thoughts
- Uses capitalization (first words of sentences and proper names) and end punctuation
- Begins to use descriptive words and writes in complete sentences
- Generates ideas, develops drafts, and makes revisions

 # Letters to Parents

Dear Parent,

Learning how to put ideas down on paper begins before children can read. While your child is acquiring many complex skills to do this independently, this process will actually take place over the next few years. *Until the children are ready to do it on their own, I will help them write down their words through a process called dictation.*

When young children's thoughts and ideas are being recorded, it is imperative that their words be scribed EXACTLY as spoken. Therefore, their thoughts will not be edited for grammar or content. When you read stories, comments, or observations that have been dictated by your child, you can rest assured that even though the text may be grammatically incorrect or seem incomplete logically, the thought processes are very appropriate for this age group.

If interested, please consider helping your child develop critical writing skills by modeling and practicing writing at home. Encourage your child to watch you use writing in various ways: making lists, sending E-mails, writing letters and notes to family members, and so on. Talk with your child about how you move your hand from left to right on the paper when writing words and sentences. Read the words aloud to link written words to speech. Provide opportunities for your child to write, too.

Thank you for your assistance,

- ✂

Dear Parent,

Each day, the children in my classroom are encouraged to put their ideas down on paper without being restricted by grammar and spelling conventions. (That will come later in the development of writing skills.) When children learn to write words, they match sounds to the letters they know. This stage is often called *invented spelling*. When your child comes home with papers that seem to be written in another language, you can rest assured that this is exactly what I expect at this time. You may also observe play situations when your child creates scribbles that look like mock writing. On the other hand, there may be times when your child writes by copying letters or words precisely, or asks you how to spell certain words when composing a story. This is also a natural part of the development of writing skills. Enjoy this time while it lasts—this stage will pass all too soon!

You can help your child develop critical writing skills by practicing writing at home. Give your child lots of opportunities to write, such as composing a letter to a grandparent. Your child may also enjoy writing short stories by first drawing pictures to generate ideas and then writing about the pictures.

Thank you for your assistance,

Writing Basics: Mechanics

Before children can begin to create through writing, they need to know some basic mechanics. Young preschoolers and those with dexterity and fine-motor difficulties will often prefer to use writing utensils with their fists. As young children develop the motor control to hold pencils correctly, they should be encouraged to hold the writing tools in a traditional manner. This will improve the children's ability to control their pencils and will produce better letter formation and spacing.

A traditional pencil grip includes pinching the pencil between the index finger and thumb, about 1 in. (25 mm) from the tip of the pencil lead. The side of the tip of the middle finger presses against the underside of the pencil for support. The fourth and fifth fingers curl under and support the hand while writing. Children who write with their left hands push their pencils along the paper (rather than pulling their pencils like right-handed writers) and often struggle to see what they are writing. Have those writers experiment with tilting their papers and gripping their pencils farther from the tips to avoid having to hook their hands over the top of their writings.

If a child struggles to hold a writing tool correctly, has difficulty controlling the pressure when making marks, and/or cannot seem to use fluid movements, you may consider the following strategies and activities:

- Have each child cup a cotton ball in the palm of the dominant hand while holding a pencil in the correct manner. This will help the children keep their fingers properly aligned.

- Purchase inexpensive rubber pencil grips for the children to use for gaining control and "training" their hands to hold pencils correctly.

- Locate special triangular-shaped pencils that the children can use when struggling to hold their pencils correctly.

- Give the children unsharpened pencils with pencil grips to use when writing in sand trays for practicing the proper way to grasp a writing tool.

- Provide opportunities for fine-motor development—such as gripping and manipulating small toys, molding clay into forms, printing with stamps, and using other art materials—to strengthen the muscles in the hands and fingers.

- Using their dominant hands, have the children practice making large circular motions in both clockwise and counterclockwise directions in the air, on paper with finger paint, and in sand trays.

- Have the children practice controlling watercolor markers in a precise manner by tracing over lines and shapes drawn on file folders. Include wavy and zigzag lines, as well as various shapes—circles, triangles, rectangles, squares, stars, ovals, and bursts—in different sizes that have been drawn with either solid or dotted lines. Be sure to indicate the starting point and direction of motion (either clockwise or counterclockwise) for tracing over each figure. (*Note*: It is important that all children can move writing tools in either direction smoothly.) To make the materials reusable, laminate the file folders or cover them with clear adhesive plastic. Then the file folders can be wiped clean after each use.

• Provide each child with a writing surface at the appropriate height. As the children sit in their chairs, check to be sure that their knees are bent at 90-degree angles while their feet rest flat on the floor.

• Write often with the class. Model the proper way to grasp a pencil, how writing represents spoken words, and the process of composing thoughts on paper.

• Using a watercolor marker, young children can practice writing words by tracing over the letters you have written. As a guide, indicate where to start forming each letter and the direction of the strokes.

• Have the children who struggle with spacing their written words appropriately use craft sticks or the width of a finger to determine how far apart their words should be. (*Note:* Offer this technique only to children who are developmentally ready for this skill.)

• Use big books to illustrate the conventions of print. The print in these books is easy to see, and you can easily highlight spacing and punctuation. Children can also learn that writing flows from left to right and from top to bottom on a page. Point out these features as you read aloud the text.

Writing Basics: Content

While children become comfortable with the mechanics of handwriting, they should also be encouraged to write freely about their ideas and stories. Slowly, their understanding of conventional writing skills will emerge. They will become attentive to correct spelling and proper punctuation. Also during this time, they will begin to express an interest in content. This stage of development generally occurs in kindergarten or first grade. Although some content writing skills, such as story webs and sequencing, can be introduced in preschool (if it is developmentally appropriate for the children), most of the writing experiences for preschoolers will be simple story writing (one or two sentences) and caption activities to introduce them to the writing process. As older children learn to write, they need to understand that a well-written piece includes enough information to tell the whole story.

Choosing a Topic

Plan to incorporate writing experiences into your curriculum every day. Those experiences might include the following: writing captions for art projects, signing up for center activities, writing letters to tell about classroom experiences, making lists, composing stories, journaling about science investigations, writing informational text, or creating poems. You can also use the specific ideas and writing activity suggestions included later in this book to help get the children started.

Brainstorming

For young children who are not as proficient at generating writing topics, you can offer suggestions for what to write. However, for kindergartners and first graders, try brainstorming instead.

Brainstorming encourages a child to think freely about a topic. Have the children individually write or dictate a short list of subjects they would like to write about and then select a favorite topic. Say to the child, "Tell me everything you know about [name of topic]." Write each idea on a separate index card. When several cards are filled, direct the child to arrange them in a logical order before writing the informational piece.

Drawing a Picture

Another strategy that helps children expand their thinking is to have them draw pictures before writing their stories. Some children may already work this way naturally. It is fascinating to watch how those children carefully refine their pictures by adding more details. While they draw, color, or paint, stories may also be blossoming in their minds. Those mental images can easily be transferred to paper when the pictures are finished, because the children now have ideas to share.

This technique of drawing a picture first need not only apply to writing stories. Children may also enjoy drawing pictures when journaling about personal experiences or when recording information about classroom science explorations.

Prompting

Another good way to elicit ideas is through prompting. Prompting involves asking children questions about their subjects that will encourage them to add their own words. Phrases such as, "What can we say about . . . ," "Help me write this down so I can remember what you're saying," or "Tell me about . . ." are all effective prompts to help children expand their thinking.

The W's of Writing

The W's of writing are a series of questions beginning with *who*, *what*, *when*, *where*, and *why* that help writers organize their thoughts when planning stories. Referring to the "W" questions when planning a story can also help flesh out ideas. (These are also important questions to ask after reading a book to the children. The rich conversations that emerge will foster the development of comprehension skills and help the children identify the elements of a story.) You may wish to write each of these words on a poster and display the poster prominently in your writing center for easy reference. The "W" questions are as follows:

- **Who** — The "who" of writing is the subject. Who is this story about?

- **What** — The "what" of writing is the action of the story. What happens to the subject?

- **When** and **Where** — The "when" and "where" provide the time and place of the action.

- **Why** — The "why" tells us the reason for things happening and how those things are important to the story.

Sequencing Story Events

Recognizing a logical order may take some practice. But even kindergarten and first-grade children can learn through repetition that a story needs a beginning, a middle section, and an ending. To practice, help the children identify the beginning, middle, and final events of stories that you read together as a class. It is only as you *re*read the stories that children can start to comprehend the basic story elements.

Allow these reading experiences to flow into storytelling experiences, letting young children experiment with language as they record stories on a tape recorder. It is best to decide beforehand the details about the main character, the setting of the story, and what happens to the character before allowing the children to record a sequel for a favorite book or a new story as a group activity.

Reading well-written stories, having in-depth conversations about books, and retelling familiar stories all prepare children for independent writing, as well as strengthen vocabulary development and comprehension. As you help a child write, map out the sequence of events first by asking guiding questions about the story. "What happens first?" "Then what happens?" and "How does the story end?" are all great prompts.

Reading Aloud the Writing Samples

Whenever possible, encourage your young writers to read aloud their works to you personally or to a small group of children. These experiences are invaluable to help children understand that writing is intended for an audience.

Creating a Writing Environment

To produce good writers, it is imperative to give children lots of opportunities to work with words. Here are several suggestions to encourage children to write:

- **Write every day.** Provide opportunities for every child to do some form of writing every day. This may include making lists, creating schedules, writing stories, journaling, practicing handwriting, etc. Keeping the curriculum varied will help build an interest in writing every day.

- **Saturate the environment with print.** Label common objects. Write down spoken words. Point out letters and writing as you see them throughout the day. Encourage children to identify uses of writing in their everyday lives.

- **Start a writing wall.** As the children learn to write letters and then words or sentences, have them add their writing to word strips and tack them to a writing wall. Set aside one space (such as the back side of a door) as a writing wall. Cover the area with a light-colored piece of kraft paper. Allow the children to write in this space (and this space only) whenever they want throughout the day. They may wish to write names, ideas, and feelings, or just doodle.

- **Use print that is linked to class activities.** Write down your schedule. Create lists for lining up, helper charts, labels for toy boxes, etc. Write on everything, including gift bags, book covers, T-shirts, place mats, place markers, cards, and door tags.

- **Use writing in novel ways.** Use writing at unexpected times and places.

Write the children's names to notify them of their turn to line up. Try writing directions (e.g., "Line up," or "Sit down") rather than verbalizing commands all of the time.

- **Create a writing center.** Include paper of all sorts, textures, and sizes, such as large rolls of newsprint, adding machine tape, cards, and textured or colored paper. Provide several different kinds of writing tools, such as pens, pencils, crayons, markers, stamps and ink pads, clay, and lettered cookie cutters. Keep your center interesting by changing the supplies on a regular basis.

- **Point out print.** Look for or display many different kinds of writing in your writing center. Include letters and postcards, signs, newspapers, lists, messages, menus, etc., not only in the writing center, but throughout the classroom and in other center play.

- **Engage in the children's writing.** Read along with the children as they read their writings to you. Ask questions to elicit more details, emotion, or information from a child's writing. As the children verbally describe more details, take notes and then let them use those notes to strengthen the content.

- **Start a classroom mailbox.** Encourage peer-to-peer writing (or teacher-to-peer writing) by providing a "mailbox" for the children to send notes to one another. (Don't forget to include words of encouragement from you, too!)

- **Don't overdo it.** If children are struggling with particular writing skills, do not push them to the point of frustration.

Home-to-School Link: Letter Swap

Children and adults alike always enjoy receiving personal messages. Decorate a large box or mailbox and place it in a prominent spot in the classroom. Invite parents to send a note or letter to their child at school. Then plan a special time for sharing the letters the children receive from home. Have the children write letters back to their parents and place them in the mailbox. (If appropriate, the children can also practice writing their names and addresses by addressing envelopes.) When the parents pick up their children from school, they can check the mailbox for letters. Otherwise, send the letters home with the children or via the mail. If Internet service is available, have the parents e-mail their children and vice versa.

Alternatively, set up a classroom Web page that describes classroom activities and highlights the children's writings. *Be sure to get parental approval before allowing any Internet use, and do not give out or post any personal information on your Web site.* Obtain a signed form from each family that gives permission to use the designated child's writing and/or photo on the Web page. (*Note:* Your school may already have a policy about Internet use. Check with your administration first before planning any Internet activities or drafting a permission form.) Use first names only when identifying individual works or photos on the Web site. Encourage the parents to visit the Web site with their children at home.

Dear Parent,

We have decorated a large mailbox for our classroom. To practice using our writing skills, we would love to fill it up with notes and letters from the children to their parents and from the parents to the children. We will be choosing a specific time each week to read all of the mail that has accumulated in our mailbox. I know it will be a thrill for your child to receive a quick note, a funny joke, or a special thought from you. To keep this fun activity going, you might consider choosing a specific day of the week to send in mail so that your child will receive something in the mailbox each week. You can deliver the mail to our classroom in person, send the letter in with your child to deliver, or mail it to the school. And when you are at the school, don't forget to check our mailbox for correspondence to you!

Additionally, we may be using the computer to send E-mail correspondence. Please read the attached form regarding the use of the Internet and sign where indicated to give your child permission to participate in this activity. If you prefer to write an E-mail to your child, you may send it to _____.

As always, please feel free to contact me if you have any questions.

Sincerely,

During the school year, you may consider having each child's family write a "family book." To do this, ask each person in the family to write a short paragraph or story about something he or she did that day. This can range from the mundane to activities or ideas of interest.

When the pages arrive at school, help the child compile them into a book. Add a cover page that says "[Child's name]'s Family Book." Read (or have the children read, if possible) the stories to the class during story time. You may wish to repeat this activity on several occasions throughout the year.

✂ --

Dear Parent,

One way to encourage your child's developing writing skills is to get your whole family involved in the writing process. This week we are compiling "family books." A family book is created by having each person in your family write a short paragraph or story about a personal experience. This could be something that happened today. The topics can range from the mundane to activities or ideas of interest. Be sure to have your child create a personal page at home, too. Each person's paragraph should be on a separate page and may be personalized by including an illustration if desired. You may include extended family members or close friends in this project as well.

Please have each family member complete one page and then send all of the pages to the school by _____. We will be compiling those pages into a book.

Thank you for your participation in this project. I know that this experience will not only strengthen your child's writing skills, but will also serve as a special memory to treasure.

Sincerely,

Home-to-School Link: Sleepover Fun

A sleepover with friends can be a lot of fun. For young children, bringing home the classroom mascot or a certain plush animal toy for a weekend sleepover could be a very special time.

To inform the parents about the sleepover, make a copy of the letter below and include all pertinent information. Be sure to give your mascot or stuffed animal toy a name and then send home the animal along with a completed copy of the letter. Include a small suitcase that holds a change of clothes, pajamas, a toothbrush, and a blanket. Also pack a storybook and a journal so that the mascot can "write down" things that he or she did while at each child's home. Have the host child record the mascot's ideas in the journal.

If interested, provide a disposable camera so your classroom mascot can have a picture taken with each host family.

You might wish to consider sending animal toys to two or three children's homes each weekend so that the children will not have to wait several months for the special visit. After the sleepovers have been completed, store the journals in your classroom library for the children to enjoy reading over and over again.

- ✂ - -

Dear Parent,

Today your child is bringing home _____ for a special weekend sleepover visit. Your child has been given suggestions for how to entertain and keep _____ happy during the visit.

In _____'s suitcase you will find a change of clothes (in case things get messy!), a pair of pajamas, a toothbrush, a blanket, and a favorite storybook. Please return all items in the suitcase when your child brings _____ back to school on Monday morning.

Feel free to take our mascot with you on family activities and outings away from home, and have your child read to the mascot each night before bed. Most importantly, please help your child write down each day's activities in first person (as if _____ is writing) in the journal provided. (Example: "Dear Journal, Today I visited Benny's house. We played baseball in the backyard. It was exciting when Benny hit a home run and I got to slide into home plate.") We will be sharing _____'s journal entries with the class on Monday. If desired, use the camera in the suitcase to take one or two pictures of your child with our mascot (or include your own digital prints) to illustrate the activities your child will be writing about in the journal. We will develop the pictures in a few weeks when the camera is full and add the pictures to the journal at that time.

Sincerely,

Home-to-School Link: Scoop Dog

Scoop Dog is a newspaper reporter. His job is to find interesting stories every day and then write about them for *The Weekly Sentinel.* Purchase or locate an inexpensive plush dog toy. You may want to outfit him with a small visor and vest. Place the dog along with copies of the completed instructions below and the form on page 17 in a small tote bag.

Send Scoop Dog home with a different child each week. After every child has had an opportunity to take Scoop Dog home and has returned with a story, publish the stories in a classroom newspaper. Share the stories with the children throughout the day of publication and then send home a newspaper with each child.

- ✂

Dear Parent,

Today your child brought home Scoop Dog, resident newspaper reporter for our classroom newspaper, *The Weekly Sentinel.* Scoop Dog's job is to write a story about your family. This may cover an activity or event that has happened in your home this week, a funny or interesting story about your family (places you have visited, things you have done, things you like to do together, etc.), or any other idea or event your child would like Scoop Dog to report about.

Scoop Dog will need your child's assistance to write the report. To begin, help your child determine the main elements by discussing ideas for the beginning, middle, and end of the story. Have your child write down the story (or dictate the story to you) on the page provided and then illustrate it with a picture in the designated box. (The illustration may be your child's own drawing, a photograph, or a picture clipped out of a magazine.)

Please return Scoop Dog and the completed newspaper page to me by _____. If you have any questions, please contact me at school. You will receive a copy of our classroom newspaper after it has been published.

Sincerely,

Scoop Dog's Form

To the Parent: Please help your child write a short story for Scoop Dog on this form.

The Weekly Sentinel

Picture

Story (as told by _____)

Making Mini-Books

Whether stapling a couple of pages together or creating a fanciful bound volume, children love creating their own books. The following pages contain directions for different kinds of books that you can make for children to use when recording their stories.

Three-Page Accordion Book — This simple mini-book is made with just one sheet of paper.

1. Fold a letter- or legal-sized piece of paper in half lengthwise, so it looks like a hot dog.
2. Fold that strip in half vertically.
3. With the last fold on the left, fold the top right edge (the paper is doubled) toward that center fold.
4. Turn the paper over and also fold that right edge toward the middle fold. (See diagram A.)
5. Staple the two folded edges together as shown to create your mini-book. (See diagram B.)

A (Step 4)

B (Step 5)

Staple the folds together to make the spine.

Four-Page Book — This simple mini-book also is made with just one sheet of paper.

1. Fold your sheet of paper as directed in the Three-Page Accordion Book instructions. Follow steps 1–4. *Do not staple the edge*.
2. Open the paper and make a slit along the lengthwise fold between the first and fourth sections. (See diagram C.)
3. Refold the paper in half as shown. Pinch the two middle folds (see diagrams D and E) and gently pull them out and toward the left.
4. Stack all of the folded sections together and staple along the edge. (See diagram F.)

C (Step 2)

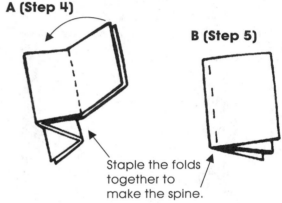

D (Step 3)

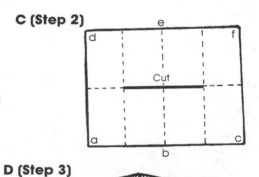

E (Step 3)

F (Step 3)

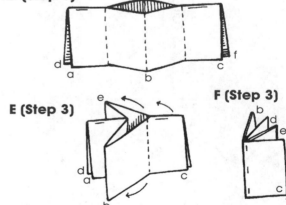

Paper Bag Book — This book can be large or small, depending on the size of the paper bags that are used.

1. Open up two paper bags and cut off the bottom of each one. Also trim off the tops to make clean edges. (See diagram A.)
2. Flatten each bag. Glue the bottom and top openings closed to make flat booklet pages. (See diagram B.) Alternatively, the edges of the bags can be left open to hold an "About the Author" page, illustrations that slide out between the pages, etc.
3. Stack the two bags on top of one another and then fold them in half the short way. Staple along the fold.
4. Glue 6 in. (15 cm) pieces of ribbon to the front and back flaps. (See diagram C.) Tie the ribbons together to keep the book closed.

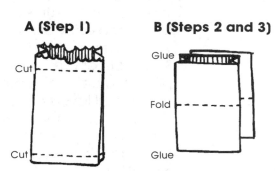

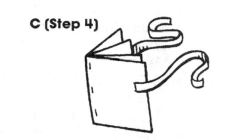

Backbone Bend Book — This technique is great when you need a book bound quickly without using a stapler.

1. Cut two or three sheets of paper in half.
2. Stack the papers on top of one another and then fold the stack in half.
3. Snip or tear through all layers of paper about $1/2$ in. (13 mm) into the folded edge of the paper. (See diagram D.)
4. Make a second snip or tear near the bottom of the page. (See diagram D.)
5. Press the middle section of the fold toward the back of the book and the small end tabs toward the front of the book. (See diagram E.)
6. Use tape or glue to secure these flaps if desired. (See diagram F.)

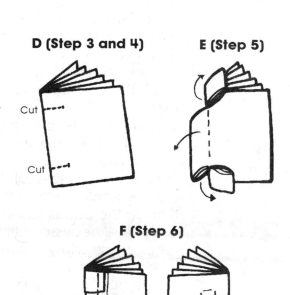

Shaped Book — Any shape or pattern page illustration can be turned into a shaped book.
1. Make one copy of the picture or shape you wish to use.
2. Stack four or five blank pages behind the picture. Staple (or secure with a metal brad) through all layers of paper.
3. Cut through all thicknesses of paper along the outline of the illustration to give the book a recognizable shape. (See illustration on right.)

Bound Book — Produce a real, bound book covered with fabric by following the steps below:
1. Cut two pieces of cardboard that are slightly larger than your book-page size.
2. Cut two pieces of quilt batting the same size as the cardboard. Glue one to each cardboard piece.
3. Lay a piece of fabric facedown on the table. Place the two pieces of cardboard, batting side down, side by side on the fabric. Leave a small gap about 1/8 in. (3 mm) between the cardboard pieces. (See diagram A.)
4. Cut the fabric 1 in. (25 mm) longer and wider than the edges of the cardboard pieces.
5. Stretch the fabric over the cardboard edges and secure with hot glue. (See diagram B.)
6. Make a stack of several sheets of paper. Fold the stack in half to make a guide for stitching the pages to the cover (as directed in step 7). If necessary, trim so that the pages are smaller than the cardboard book cover.
7. Lay the pages on top of the cardboard cover. Carefully stitch down the middle of the papers and the cover with a sewing machine. Be sure to use craft thread and a long stitch. (See diagram C.)
8. Glue the first page of the book to the inside front cover and the last page to the inside back cover to hide the ragged edges of the fabric. Add a ribbon bookmark if desired.

A (Step 3)

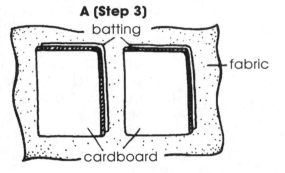

batting

fabric

cardboard

B (Step 5)

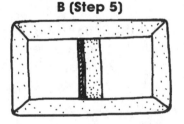

C (Step 7)

Stick in the Mud

Materials

- 9 x 13 in. (23 x 33 cm) baking pans
- assortment of twigs and old tree branches
- card stock
- chart paper
- glue
- mud
- thick spaghetti
- thin dowels
- water
- water table or large, shallow plastic container

Skill Builders

- finger dexterity
- letter recognition

Getting Ready

- Prepare mud for a water or sensory table, or fill a shallow plastic container with it. Make sure the mud is soft enough for writing, but firm enough to hold the shape of written letters.
- Gather several sticks or old tree branches. Cut or snap the branches into short sticks.

Extending the Lesson

- Cut the dowels or sticks into 3 in. (8 cm) lengths. Have the children use the dowels, sticks, or spaghetti to form letters or words and glue them onto pieces of card stock.

Activity

Children may not be able to resist practicing their writing skills and playing in the mud at the same time! Ask the children to gather around a sensory table filled with mud. Demonstrate how they can create letters, shapes, and pictures by drawing in the mud with a stick. The children can easily erase their writings by rubbing or pressing the mud into a smooth surface. Encourage them to try sticks of different diameters when writing. If interested, fill a baking pan with mud and write letters, words, or names in it for the children to copy when working in the mud at the big sensory table.

Science Connection: Mud Magic

Invite the children to investigate what happens when the consistency of the mud is altered by adding water. Provide three or four baking pans filled with a thin layer of mud. Have the children write or draw in the mud and then carefully pour a small amount of water over their drawings. The children may be surprised to see that their writings disappear. (Each time more water is added, the mixture becomes thinner.) Ask, "How much water does it take before you can no longer see the writing in the mud?" (*Note:* Add more dirt to firm things up again.) Continue the lesson by having the children experiment with sand or cornstarch. *Questions to investigate*: Which substance is the best for writing? Which one holds the most water? During large group time, discuss the children's findings and record their observations on a piece of chart paper.

Sensory Writing

Materials

- blank audiotape and tape recorder
- copy paper
- cotton swabs
- crayons and pencils
- food extracts
- large baking sheet
- masking tape
- paint
- sandpaper
- shaving cream
- small paper cups

Skill Builders

- sensory awareness
- small-motor skills

Getting Ready

- Cut enough sheets of sandpaper into thirds to give each child one or more pieces.
- Tape the sandpaper sheets onto the table.
- Prepare the audiotape as directed in the language-arts connection activity.

Extending the Lesson

- Have the children paint pictures with their favorite colors or scented paint. Then ask them to write about how the fragrance makes them feel or about things that have the same scent. (*Note:* Some children may only be able to write or dictate a caption.)

Activity

Expand the writing center to include writing activities that engage the senses of smell, touch, and sound. Not only will you appeal to the children's senses by engaging more than one sense at a time, but it is also a good way to teach basic mechanics of writing.

Smell — Pour a small amount of paint into a paper cup. Add a few drops of a food extract or essential oil to the cup to give the paint a distinct scent. Repeat with other paint colors and scents. Have the children dip cotton swabs into the scented paints and write letters or words on their papers.

Touch — Place a dollop of shaving cream on a large baking sheet or the table. Spread the shaving cream across the surface to cover it. Encourage the children to use their fingers to write or draw in the shaving cream palate. To erase their writings, they can just rub across the top of the shaving cream.

Sound — Tape sheets of sandpaper (use several different grit samples) to the table. Place a piece of copy paper on top of the sandpaper. Using crayons or pencils, the children can write letters and words or draw pictures on the paper. When they write on the paper, can they hear a noise? Also have the children try writing directly on pieces of sandpaper, using a different writing tool each time. Does the type of writing utensil used make a difference?

Language-Arts Connection: Listen and Follow

Make an audiotape of writing suggestions. Example: Sing part of the alphabet song and then stop. Instruct the child to write the letter that comes next. Continue this exercise for several other letters. Alternatively, sing familiar Mother Goose rhymes. Have the children write down the missing rhyming words.

My Name Is Special

Materials

- chart paper
- colored card stock
- copy paper
- index cards
- large bowl
- markers
- recorded musical selection and audiotape or CD player
- stapler
- word strips

Skill Builders

- name recognition

Getting Ready

- Create an autograph book for each child by folding several sheets of copy paper in half. Then fold a piece of card stock in half. Slip the card stock over the copy paper to create a cover for the autograph book. Form the book by stapling along the fold. Write "My Autograph Book" on the cover and leave a space for the child's name.
- Write each child's name on a separate word strip and also on an index card.
- Write your name on a word strip.

Activity

Helping children connect letters of the alphabet with the letters used to spell names is a great way to build early literacy skills. Show the children the word strip with your name written on it. Find out if any of the children can identify the name on the card. Talk about how everyone's name is unique—just like every person. Have the children close their eyes and then ask them, "When we say [child's name], what does that make you think about?" The children should give responses that describe or tell about the child you have named. Repeat the exercise with the other children's names.

Hold up one of the prepared name strips, for example "José." Ask that child to come up and write his name on the chart paper. Have him point to and read aloud each letter in his name. Next, encourage the child to lead the class in a small movement activity, such as jumping up and down or clapping hands. Repeat the procedure until all of the children have had an opportunity to lead. Give each child an autograph book. Encourage the children to get the autograph of everyone in the class.

Extending the Lesson

Show the children different ways to write their names, including block lettering and cursive. Have them experiment by writing their names in a variety of ways. (*Note*: You may want to print out a sheet produced on the computer that shows the child's name written with various fonts as examples.)

Music Connection: Name Match

With this fun activity, young children will start to recognize other children's names. Prior to the lesson, be sure each child's name is printed on an index card. Fold the cards in half and place them in a large bowl. Play a favorite musical selection as the children mill about or dance. When the music stops, have each child select a name from the bowl. The children must find the people named on their cards and shake hands with them. When everyone is finished, have the children return the cards to the bowl and then start the music again.

Letter Detective

Materials

- card stock
- copy paper
- kraft paper
- pattern page 25
- pencils
- real magnifying glass
- safety pins
- tape
- various examples of print
- watercolor marker

Skill Builders

- letter recognition
- awareness of print in the environment

Getting Ready

- Display different kinds of print around the room.
- Make a copy of the Letter Detective pattern page onto heavy card stock for each child. Have the children color and cut out each item.
- Attach a detective badge to each child with a safety pin.
- Cut a piece of copy paper into fourths. Staple several pages to the back side of the logbook cover. On the first page, include a copy of the letters that the children are directed to find. Trim edges as necessary.
- Cut out the center of each child's spyglass.

Activity

Letters can be found everywhere. For this activity, have the children become "letter detectives." As detectives, they must use clues when investigating their case. They must examine things closely, just like real detectives do. Their job is to search for hidden or missing letters. They can use their "spyglasses" if desired or a real magnifying glass. Have the children take their logbooks on a search for every letter of the alphabet or just for preselected letters. They may have to look high, low, around corners, and in tight spots to find the letters. Once they have spotted a letter, they should copy it into their logbooks. (*Note*: More than one letter can be written on each page.) Also have the children cross off the found letter on the first page of their logbooks.

Extending the Lesson

If your children are proficient at letter recognition, add this twist to the activity. Write the title "What's Your Alibi?" across the top of a piece of paper. Then use the spyglass pattern to decorate the page. Tell the children that they are all suspects in a crime. In order to prove themselves innocent, the children must provide alibis by each making a list of everything they did during that day. Once the lists are complete, you can rule out all suspects in the case.

Music Connection: Who Took the Letter?

Have all of the children sit in a circle. Tape a large sheet of kraft paper to the floor. Using the tune of "Who Stole the Cookies from the Cookie Jar?" have the children sing while alternately tapping their knees and clapping their hands. Example:

Class: "Who took the [A] from our alphabet?"
Then call out a name [for example, Cindy] and sing, "Cindy took the *A* from our alphabet!"
Cindy: "Who, me?"
Class: "Yes, you!"
Cindy: "Maybe!"
Class: "Put it back!"

Cindy would then write the letter *A* on the paper. Continue singing and calling out names until the entire alphabet is written on the paper.

ABC
DEFGHIJKLMNOPQRSTUVW
XYZ

My Logbook

Name _____

Set Sail with Games

Materials

- blue file folders
- glue
- pattern page 27
- scissors
- self-adhesive plastic or laminating film
- watercolor markers

Skill Builders

- finger dexterity
- letter recognition
- writing practice

Getting Ready

- Make copies of the sailboat patterns as directed for each activity. (*Note*: Copy the patterns onto colored paper or decorate them with markers.)
- Glue the sailboats onto the inside of a file folder as directed for each game.
- Write simple game instructions on paper and attach them to the front of each file folder.
- Write the name of the activity on the file-folder tab.

Extending the Lesson

- Consider making enlarged copies of the sailboats and writing simple words on the sails. Then have the children copy the words on the hulls of the sailboats.

Activity

Making Waves

Make two copies of the sailboat pattern page. Paste half of the sailboats down the left-hand side of the opened file folder. Draw colorful stars on those sails to remind the children about where to start the activity. Glue the other sailboats down the right-hand side of the file folder. Draw dotted, wavy, zigzag, curly, and 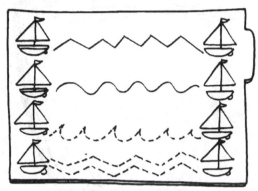 straight lines between the sailboats. Decorate the sailboats as desired. Laminate or cover the file folder with self-adhesive plastic for repeated use.

To Play: Use a watercolor marker to trace the line from each sailboat on the left to the sailboat on the right. Continue until all sailboats have been connected. Clean the folder with a damp cloth before putting it away.

Matching Sails

Make two copies of the sailboat patterns. Write an uppercase letter on one part of each sail. Include a small arrow and star to show the children how to form each letter. Cut out the sailboats and glue them onto the inside of the file folder. Decorate the file folder as desired. Laminate or cover the file folder with self-adhesive plastic for repeated use.

To Play: Write the corresponding lowercase letter on the open part of each sail. Preschool children may just be able to write the uppercase letter again.

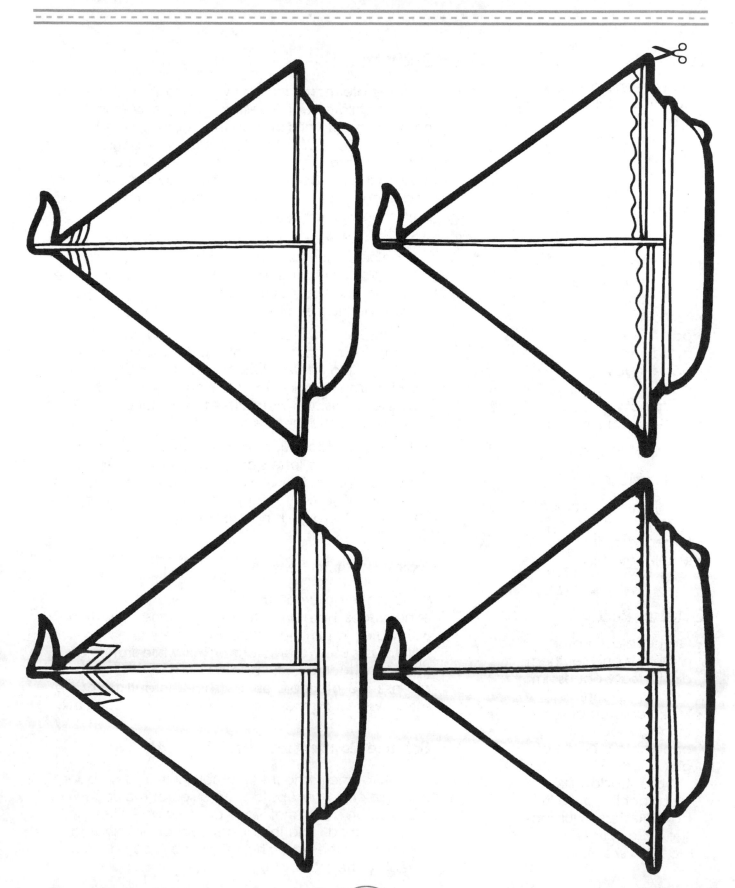

Novel Writing

Materials

- bulletin-board letters
- cotton swabs
- feathers
- food coloring
- forks
- glue
- jumbo-sized craft sticks or wooden skewers
- lamp
- lemon juice
- letter stamps
- letter-shaped cookie cutters
- lipstick
- paint
- paper
- paper cups
- pencils
- toothpicks
- water-soluble ink pads

Skill Builders

- using variety of objects to write
- finger dexterity
- small-motor skills

Getting Ready

- Gather all of the materials and set them out for easy access in the writing center.
- Make colored glue by adding food coloring or paint to a bottle of glue. Mix well.
- Create shadow sticks by attaching bulletin-board letters to jumbo-sized craft sticks or wooden skewers.

Activity

There are many different writing tools and methods that the children can investigate. First, have the children name different kinds of tools that they can use to write. Once they have listed things like pencils, pens, markers, chalk, and crayons, ask them to think of other things they could use. Demonstrate the following examples and encourage the children to try a different idea each day in the writing center:

- Provide ink pads or small cups of paint and a variety of objects, such as cotton swabs, feathers, forks, toothpicks, and craft sticks. Dip one end of the object into the paint or press it onto the ink pad and then write your name or draw a picture with the object.

- Place several water-soluble ink pads along with letter stamps, letter-shaped cookie cutters, and pencils in the writing center. Press a letter stamp or cookie cutter onto the ink pad and then onto the paper to create letters and words. Use the eraser or your finger to create dotted letters and words.

- Use unusual tools such as lipstick or colored glue to write words and letters on paper. (Twist the tip of the glue bottle so that just a small amount of glue is released when squeezing the bottle.) Allow the glue to dry before displaying the paper.

Extending the Lesson

Take the children outside for different writing experiences. Here are a few suggestions: Try writing with water by printing letters on a sidewalk with a wet paintbrush. Use watercolor markers while standing in the rain. Attach bulletin-board letters to craft sticks that are inserted into the ground. Trace the outlines of the shadows cast on sheets of paper with colored chalk.

Science Connection: Invisible Ink

Pour a small amount of lemon juice into a paper cup. Use cotton swabs to write a secret message with the juice on a piece of white copy paper. After the juice has dried, hold the paper over an illuminated lightbulb. As the paper heats up, the juice will burn, revealing the message!

Roll and Print

Materials

- 3 or 4 lettered dice
- index cards
- paper
- pencils
- plastic container with lid
- standard dice
- watercolor marker
- word cards
- word strips

Skill Builders

- letter recognition
- writing letters of the alphabet

Getting Ready

- Create a set of alphabet flash cards by writing each letter on a separate index card.

Extending the Lesson

- Encourage first graders to think of words that begin with the letters that are rolled. For example, if the letter *F* is drawn and the number *3* is rolled, the child should then write three words that begin with that letter. Write those words on word strips and display them on an alphabet word wall. Continue by playing several rounds to generate words. If appropriate, have the children play the game during free time to add more words to the display.

Activity

Shake, roll, and print letters for extra practice! Give each child a piece of paper and a pencil. Place three or four lettered dice in a plastic container and seal it with a lid. Have one child shake the container and then roll the dice onto the table. Direct the child to read aloud the letters shown on the dice so that the other children can write those letters on their papers. Continue shaking, rolling, and writing until the papers are filled with letters.

Alternatively, scatter a set of alphabet flash cards facedown on the table. Have the children take turns drawing a letter card and rolling a numbered die. For example, if the letter *P* is drawn and the number *5* is rolled on the die, the children should write the letter *P* five times.

Large-Motor Connection: Roll and Bend

Let's move our bodies to make letter shapes! Use the same set of lettered dice for this activity. Have the children stand in a large open area. Choose one child to roll a die on the floor. All of the children then identify the letter shown and try to make the shape of that letter with their bodies. If necessary, they can lie on the floor or join a friend to create the letter shape.

 # Pictographs

Materials

- adhesive bandage
- clip-art pictures
- dice
- egg cartons
- glue stick and scissors
- paper
- pattern page 31
- pictures of hieroglyphics
- pictures of icons, such as men/women restroom signs, etc.
- red construction paper
- tablecloth, watercolor markers, kraft paper and tape

Skill Builders

- writing skills
- pictures convey meaning

Getting Ready

- Use red paper to make an octagon shape.
- Make several copies of the pattern page. Cut along the dashed lines to separate the pictures. Store the sets of matching pictures in egg-cartons.

Extending the Lesson

- Discuss ancient hieroglyphics. Cover a table with a heavy cloth. Tape a sheet of kraft paper to the underside of the table. Invite the children to make "hieroglyphics" on the paper while inside the "cave."

Activity

Begin by talking about how pictures sometimes take the place of words. Show the children the red octagon. Ask them, "What does this mean?" (More than likely the children will express that what you are holding is a stop sign.) Even though the word *STOP* is not printed on the octagon, the color and shape make the octagon meaningful. Next, hold up the adhesive bandage and ask again, "What does this mean?" (The bandage is associated with "boo-boos" and pain.) Finally, draw a heart shape on paper and ask the children, "What does this mean?" (A heart will generally remind children of love.)

In various places symbols (graphics) are used to represent words. Show examples of wordless icons (restroom signs, etc.) and ask the children to explain what the pictures mean. Hold up several of the small pictures provided on the pattern page and have the children tell you what each picture represents. Create a short sentence with the pictures to demonstrate to the children how to write without words.

In the writing center, encourage the children to create their own rebus stories by gluing pictures onto their papers. Alternatively, clip pictures from magazines for the rebus stories. During circle time, invite the children to share their stories.

Math Connection: Count-and-Paste Game

Preschoolers will delight in counting up to six and pasting pictures on their own game boards. Using copies of the pattern page, select eight pictures for each game board. Glue the pictures in a vertical column down the left-hand edge of a sheet of paper. Draw a box next to each picture.

To play, give each pair of children a die, two game boards, and a glue stick. Have them decide who starts the game. The first player rolls the die, counts the dots shown, and writes the corresponding numeral in the box next to the first picture on her game board. She then glues that same number of matching pictures in the first row next to the box. The players take turns rolling the die and gluing pictures until their game boards are complete.

Picture the Day

Materials

- card stock
- constuction paper or patterned scrapbook paper
- digital camera
- glue or photo-mount adhesive
- objects to photograph
- watercolor markers

Skill Builders

- words convey meaning
- expressing stories about personal experiences
- using descriptive language

Getting Ready

- Two or three days before making the scrapbook, take pictures that represent every activity of the day. Be sure to take at least one photograph of each child individually or working with others on tasks. Events may include the following:
  - arriving at school
  - placing objects in lockers or cubbies
  - play time
  - circle time or morning meeting
  - outside play
  - lunch
  - rest time
  - center time
  - going home
- Make 5 in. x 7 in. (13 cm x 18 cm) prints of the photographs.

Activity

Create lasting memories with a picture book of classroom activities. Let each child select a personal picture from the collection of classroom photographs and a sheet of special paper. Direct the children to mount their pictures on the paper, leaving space at the bottom for writing. (If dark-colored or patterned paper is used, cut an additional piece of white or light-colored paper and mount it below the photograph.)

Have the child study the picture for a moment. Then ask, "What is happening in this picture?" As the child responds, record the text in narrative form. For example, if Kayla tells you, "It's me! I'm playing blocks," you can help her reword the description. Guide her by saying, "This is Kayla. She is playing with the blocks." Write the dictated sentence below the picture. Allow the child to create a decorative border around the page. Once all of the pages have been completed, compile them into a book—a classroom scrapbook!

Extending the Lesson

Make sequencing activities using photographs of the class. As the children work on various projects, take photographs to show their progress from beginning to end. Mount the pictures on pieces of construction paper and assemble them into a booklet. Have the children dictate their stories to you, which are recorded below the pictures. Later, read aloud the stories during circle time. The children may enjoy predicting what will happen next before turning the page to see the results.

Math Connection: Numbers and Counting

1, 2, 3 . . . How many things can you see? Children will enjoy selecting objects in the classroom to make a picture book about numbers. First, arrange the chosen objects on a plain background. Using an aerial view, take photographs that show the objects in number sets, such as pictures of one dog, two cars, and three trucks. Mount each picture on a piece of card stock, leaving space at the bottom for writing. Have the children help you write a caption for each page. Then display the picture book in the math center for free exploration.

List It!

Materials

- chart paper and markers
- items to create a grocery store in the dramatic-play center
- pattern page 34

Skill Builders

- alternate forms of writing

Getting Ready

- Create a few sample lists, such as a grocery list, top 10 TV shows for children, professional sports teams, and household chores.
- Generate a list of art supplies that the children can use during center time. Write those items on the pattern page and then make copies for the children to use.

Extending the Lesson

- Give the children a topic, such as "Things found in a garden" or "Things to do outside," and have them create their own list of 10 things. Compile all of the lists into a classroom "Top Ten" book. Add this book to your classroom library or share the lists with the children during circle time or reading instruction time.

Activity

Not every piece of writing is a story. Sometimes people may need to pass on information by making lists. A list is a group of words that all have a similar purpose or theme. Show the children a grocery list. Say, "This writing is not a story, but it does give me a lot of information. It tells me exactly what to buy when I get to the store." Discuss how all of the items on that list can be purchased at a grocery store. Then talk about other kinds of lists, such as a list of chores a person wants to do or a list of things that people feel are important. Read the lists that you have created and see if the children can discern the purpose or theme of each one. Finally, create lists with the children, such as the daily schedule, a sign-up sheet for a center, or a class roster. Create a new list on chart paper every day for a few days and display each one in a prominent location.

Tell the children that they are going to create their own lists. Make several copies of the pattern page, cut apart the patterns, and leave them in the writing center for the children to use. Possible topics for the children might include names of friends, names of immediate and extended family members, names of favorite foods, and favorite things to do on vacation.

Provide a materials list for the art center. Have the children check off the types of art supplies on the list that they wish to use. Lists for other classroom activities could also be created and used by the children.

Role-Play Connection: Let's Shop!

Set up a grocery store in the dramatic-play area. First, gather an assortment of food containers and boxes, as well as plastic fruits and vegetables. Place these items on shelves. If possible, add a shopping cart, a cash register, shopping bags, aprons for store workers, wallets and purses, pretend money, and anything else needed to complete your grocery store. Encourage the children to look at store flyers for pricing the various items. Have them make signs by cutting out pictures from flyers or writing messages on paper. Create several short shopping lists for the children to use. When the children are ready to shop, have them pick up a list and purchase only those designated items.

 # List It! Patterns

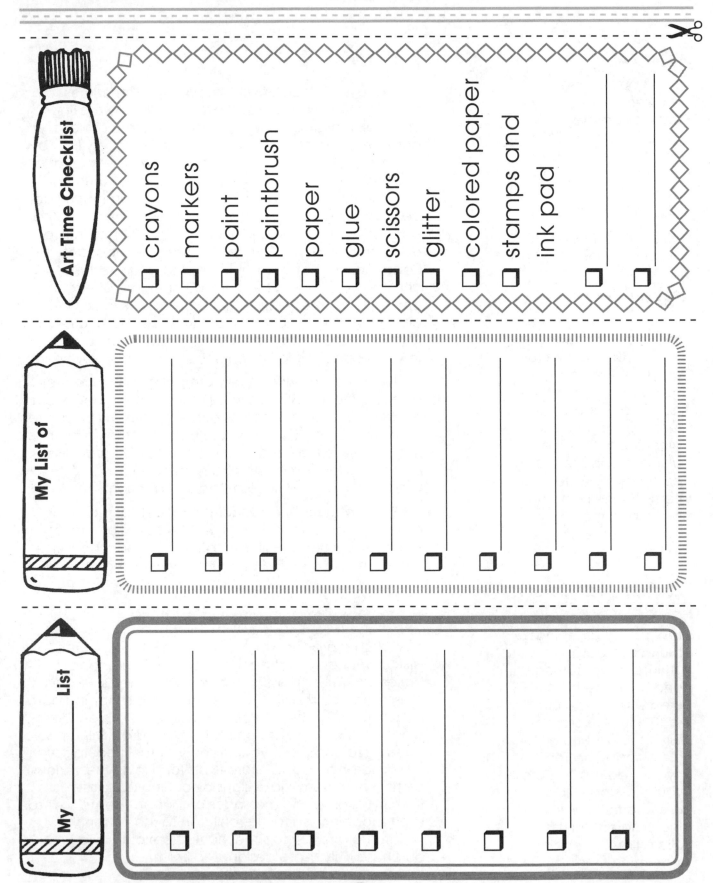

Art Time Checklist

- ☐ crayons
- ☐ markers
- ☐ paint
- ☐ paintbrush
- ☐ paper
- ☐ glue
- ☐ scissors
- ☐ glitter
- ☐ colored paper
- ☐ stamps and ink pad
- ☐ _____
- ☐ _____

My List of _____

- ☐ _____
- ☐ _____
- ☐ _____
- ☐ _____
- ☐ _____
- ☐ _____
- ☐ _____
- ☐ _____
- ☐ _____
- ☐ _____

My _____ List

- ☐ _____
- ☐ _____
- ☐ _____
- ☐ _____
- ☐ _____
- ☐ _____
- ☐ _____
- ☐ _____

 # Author of the Day

Materials

- crayons
- envelopes, index cards, and other equipment needed to set up a library play center
- fabric or blanket to cover the author's chair
- favorite picture books
- paper
- pattern pages 36 and 37
- scissors and tape
- stapler

Skill Builders

- book awareness
- listening for details

Getting Ready

- Prepare book pages by cutting several sheets of paper to the desired size. Ideas for making a variety of mini-books are also provided on pages 18–20.
- Use the pattern pages to make one crown and one certificate for each child. Also cut paper lengthwise to make a long paper strip for each child.

Extending the Lesson

- Every few weeks, set aside one day as "Picture-book Author Day." On that day, read aloud several published books by the same author.

Activity

Encourage the children to become authors by writing and illustrating their own books. Share some favorite books with the children by reading them aloud. Then talk about the various elements of a book: the cover, the title page, the publisher's name, the copyright page, the dedication, the story pages, and the page numbers. Discuss with the children their ideas for their own books. Ask guiding questions to help them decide if their writings will be about personal experiences, make-believe stories, or factual pieces. If some children are interested in a specific science topic, such as dinosaurs or bears, read an informational book together to prepare them for that type of writing experience. After the children have completed their writings, compile their pages into books.

During a designated time each day, invite one of the children to be the "Author of the Day." Give that child a copy of the author's crown to decorate as desired. Glue the crown to a paper strip. Wrap the strip around the child's head, taping the ends together to secure them in place. Cover the special author's chair with a fun piece of fabric or luxurious  blanket. Then have the "author" sit in the chair, while wearing the crown, and read the featured story. If you are working with preschool or kindergarten children, just let them pretend to "read" their stories if they are confident enough to do this. Even though they may only have mock writing on their papers, they could be quite capable of telling a complete story.

After the featured story is read, allow the audience an opportunity to ask the author questions or share something they liked about the story. When the discussion is finished, invite the audience to walk up to a small table for a REVERSE book signing. In this case, the children who listened to the story now can sign the author's book and talk with the author individually. Leave space on the back of the book jacket/cover for this purpose. After everyone has signed the book, present the author with the special certificate.

Role-Playing Connection: Going to the Library

Set up a special library in the dramatic-play area by displaying certain book titles on a shelf or table. If appropriate, give each book a number or letter to make it easier for the "librarian" to arrange the books numerically or alphabetically on the tables. If needed, write each number or letter on a label and affix it to the table. Have the children use the labels as a guide when sorting the books into groups. On the back of each book, attach an envelope to create a pocket. Write the name of the book on an index card, placing it inside the pocket. Set up a second table for checking out books.

The "librarian" can pretend to scan the book and then stamp the current date on each book's card, giving it to the borrower. Before checking out, each child signs a small card to make a personal library card.

Encourage the children to schedule and plan a story hour in their "library play center." Perhaps one child would like to be the storyteller during that special library time.

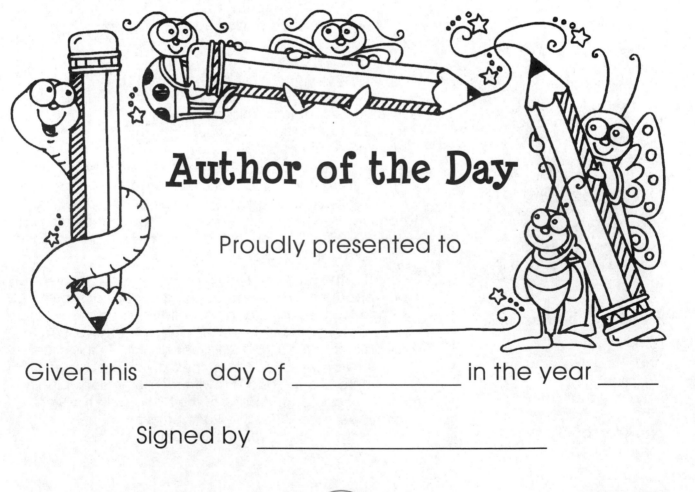

Author of the Day

Proudly presented to

_____

Given this _____ day of _____ in the year _____

Signed by _____

Author of the Day

Label Attack

Materials

- index cards
- music and audiotape or CD player
- peel-and-stick notepaper
- watercolor markers

Skill Builders

- words have meaning

Getting Ready

- Prepare a set of labels for common classroom objects, such as door, table, chair, and rug.
- Prepare a second set of labels with the children's names written on them.

Extending the Lesson

- Encourage the children to identify objects that have been previously labeled with a secondary characteristic. For example, a wooden table could also be labeled with the word *wood*. An orange could also be labeled with the word *food* or *fruit*. See how many dual labels the children can create.

Activity

Every object in the classroom has a name or word associated with it. Talk about the names of objects that the children see. For example, the round can for storing garbage is called a "trash can" or "wastepaper basket." Introduce the prepared labels for classroom objects. Encourage the children to look closely at the letters that are used to spell the words. Talk about their sounds. Then allow the children individually to choose a label and affix it to the corresponding object. Continue labeling objects as time and interest allow. Introduce a few labels each day, depending on the children's skill level.

Show the children the labels with their names printed on them. Explain that just like objects, they have words (or names) that identify them. Call the children up one at a time and stick their name labels on them.

In the writing center, provide lots of blank peel-and-stick notepaper and markers so the children can continue the activity and label other objects around the classroom. (It is recommended to use peel-and-stick notepaper to make cleanup a little easier.)

Math Connection: Label Walk

Here is a fun suggestion to practice identifying the numerals 0–5 or 0–10, depending on the developmental level of the children. Decide the range of numbers to feature and then write each one on a separate index card. If needed, include a set of dots with each numeral for identification purposes. Prepare one complete set of numeral cards for each player. Arrange the cards faceup randomly on the floor in a large open area. Play some music and have the children march in a circle around the cards. After awhile, stop the music and call out a number. Each player must then find the corresponding numeral to stand on. Continue the game until all of the numbers have been found by the children. Vary the experience by having the children jump, tiptoe, or hop while waiting for the number to be called.

Writing "Recipes"

Materials

- 3 paper bags
- favorite food recipe and necessary ingredients
- large index cards and chart paper
- scissors and markers
- some additional ingredients not included in the recipe

Skill Builders

- alternate forms of writing

Getting Ready

- Copy a recipe onto the poster board or chart paper.
- Cut index cards in half for the large-motor connection activity.

Extending the Lesson

- Expand the recipe concept by having the children think of recipes for other activities, such as a "Recipe for Fun." For example, the ingredients may include one sunny day, a friend, water balloons, swimsuits, and frozen fruit-flavored treats. Complete the recipe by writing the instructions for having fun. Illustrate the unique recipes and include them with food recipes in a classroom cookbook.

Activity

A recipe is a type of list that gives the reader specific information. Show the children the food recipe card you have created. First, have them help you read the list of ingredients and then find the actual ingredients from those you have gathered. Next, read aloud the instructions to help the chidren understand the steps that must be followed. Finally, have the children help you measure the ingredients and prepare the food by adding and mixing ingredients according to the recipe.

At the writing center, direct the children to compose food recipes of their choosing. To do this, have each child write down the name of the dish, a list of ingredients and quantities needed, and simple instructions for making the concoction. The children may write down (or dictate) their ideas on large index cards. When finished, photocopy and compile the food recipes to make a classroom cookbook.

Large-Motor Connection: Activity Recipes

Gather three paper bags. Write the numerals 1–10 individually on index cards and place the cards in the first bag. Record specific movement suggestions on index cards and place them in the second bag. Ideas could include "jump up and down," "skip," "spin around," "curl into a ball," "roll like a log," and "jumping jacks." Write directions such as "as fast as you can," "mix with," and so on for the third bag. Have the children draw one card from each container to start a movement recipe and then act out the directions. Continue drawing cards and performing the actions as time and interest allow.

Alternatively, prepare the movement recipes prior to the lesson. For example: Write down three movement activities, such as "five jumping jacks," "ten finger wiggles," and "three spins." Your instructions might read, "Do five jumping jacks as fast as you can. Next, stir in 10 finger wiggles, and then rest for 30 seconds. Stand up and do three spins, but don't over spin." Gather the children in a large open area and follow the recipe together. Encourage the children to create their own activity recipes for the class to perform.

Mail It

Materials

- chart paper
- copy paper
- envelopes
- index cards
- paper bags
- pencils, crayons, and watercolor markers
- postcards
- stamps

Skill Builders

- writing as a means of communication
- learning names and addresses

Getting Ready

- Gather a list of all the children's mailing addresses.
- Make copies of the letter template.
- Duplicate copies of the postcard template onto card stock.
- Ask parents to mail postcards to the school for their children to receive. Display them in the writing center.

Extending the Lesson

- First graders can create postcards with the template on page 42. Have the children draw pictures on the back sides of their postcards. On each card front, the child can write a short note and the recipient's address before affixing a stamp and mailing it.

Activity

One way to communicate with others is through writing letters or postcards. Many years ago, before we could communicate by computer or even phone, information was sent via mail service.

Discuss with first graders the basic rules to remember when writing letters. For younger children, simplify the format to make the activity appropriate. They will still enjoy sending letters to their parents. Model how to write a letter by composing one on chart paper.

Standard letter format:
- The date goes in the upper right-hand corner.
- The letter starts out with a greeting that addresses the recipient (person receiving the letter). Traditionally, letters begin with the greeting, "Dear _____".
- The body of the letter is the message to the recipient. This could be a story, a request, or personal news about the sender.
- The letter ends with a salutation or "good-bye phrase." Examples include "Sincerely," "Love," "Miss You," and "See You Soon." The salutation line closes the letter.
- Finally, the person writing the letter signs it.

Have the children use their time in the writing center to write letters to their parents. Provide copies of the letter template as a guide to help the children to remember the format of a letter. Allow younger children to use plain copy paper as stationery for their messages to parents. Mail the letters for the children.

Math Connection: Mail Scramble

Depending on the skill level of the children, determine which numbers to feature for a matching game. For example, collect 20 paper bags and label each one with a numeral (1–20) for first graders. Using small index cards, create "postcards" for the game by affixing "stamps" and drawing sets of dots or writing math sentences that correspond with the numbers (answers) shown on the bags. As an example, a preschooler could "deliver" a postcard showing a set of five dots to the bag with the numeral 5 printed on it. The game is finished when all of the cards have been delivered to the correct bags.

Letter Template

_____
(date)

Dear _____,

_____

_____

_____

_____

_____

Sincerely,

_____

 # Postcard Templates

_____

(name)

_____

(street address)

_____

(city, state, zip code)

_____

(name)

_____

(street address)

_____

(city, state, zip code)

Thematic Dictionary

Materials

- alphabet flash cards
- copy paper
- crayons or watercolor markers
- glue
- magazine or clip-art pictures
- scissors
- stapler

Skill Builders

- letter recognition

Getting Ready

- Cut several sheets of copy paper in half. Stack seven half sheets on top of one another. Fold the stack of paper in half and then staple the pages together along the fold to create a book. Write "My _____ Dictionary" on the front cover of the book. Make a book for each child in class.

Extending the Lesson

- Encourage the children to add definitions and use the featured words in sentences. For example: "Q — Quickly. Quickly means to move fast. The ants move quickly across the ground."
- Consider having the children copy the "word of the day" on the appropriate page in their books.

Activity

Create word topic dictionaries for any theme or unit the children are studying. For example, during your unit on insects, have the child write "Insect" on the line provided on the cover page. Then have the child write each letter of the alphabet on the top of a page—one letter per page. As the children learn about a certain topic, they can add related words to their dictionaries. For example, to fill in the insect dictionary, the child would write the word *ant* on the letter A page, use the word in a sentence, and draw a picture of an ant. For the letter *B*, the child could enter the word *bee*, and so on. When the children are ready to complete a page, have each child tell you a sentence. If appropriate, draw a blank for each word as you repeat the sentence and then have the child fill in the blanks. This process will help young children see the relationship between spoken words and print. For children who are learning to identify the letters of the alphabet, write those letters on the pages for them. Those children may enjoy making alphabet books about animals. Preschoolers may only be capable of copying the letters or drawing pictures of related objects.

Large-Motor Connection: Alphabet Rumble

Place all of the letters from an alphabet flash-card set faceup on the floor in the middle of a large open area. At your signal, have a child run to the middle of the circle and find a specific letter in the alphabet. For example, after Megan locates the correct card for the letter *L*, she names a word that begins with that letter. If the answer is correct, the other children make as much noise as possible with their hands and feet. Collect the card and then announce a different letter for another child to find. Continue until every child has located a letter.

Sequencing Stories

Materials

- chart paper
- construction paper
- copy paper
- crayons
- pattern pages 45–47
- peel-and-stick notepaper
- picture books
- scissors and glue
- watercolor markers

Skill Builders

- identifying first/middle/ end events in stories
- sequencing events

Getting Ready

- Make one copy of the picture pattern pages for each child.
- Separate the stories along the solid midline.
- Cut several pieces of colored construction paper lengthwise into thirds to create long strips of paper.

Extending the Lesson

- Let the children choose favorite books. Give each child three sheets of peel-and-stick notepaper. Write the words *beginning*, *middle*, and *end* on the papers. Have the children place the notepapers in their books to mark the corresponding parts. Sit down with the children individually and discuss their labels.

Activity

Gather a small group of children and read aloud a favorite picture book that they have heard several times. (*Note:* Choose a story with three main events that are easy for the children to identify.) After reading the story, ask the children which part came first. When the group reaches a consensus, ask the children to identify the middle part of the story. Finally, have the children explain the ending of the story. Talk about how all good writing has a beginning, middle, and an end. Have the children help you generate an original short story by mapping out the beginning, middle, and end events. Write any pertinent information on chart paper. Then have the children dramatize the story while you tell it.

In the writing center, place copies of the story sequencing patterns, the strips of construction paper, scissors, glue, crayons, and watercolor markers. Have the children each choose one sequence story to color. Direct the children to separate the images by cutting along the dashed lines between the pictures. Then have them glue the pictures in the correct order onto the construction paper strips. Finally, have the children write the story that is portrayed by the pictures. Alternatively, you may wish to have the children tell you each sentence. Repeat the sentences aloud as you write the words for the child.

Using the blank sequencing template or copy paper, have the children write and illustrate their own stories. Share the stories during reading time.

Role-Play Connection: Act It Out

Use one of your sequencing stories for a simplified three-act play. Invite the children to work in teams to create costumes, gather props, and establish the set as needed. Then have the children perform the stories for an audience. The first act represents the beginning of the story, the second act tells the middle part of the story, and the third act is the end of the story.

Story Picture Patterns

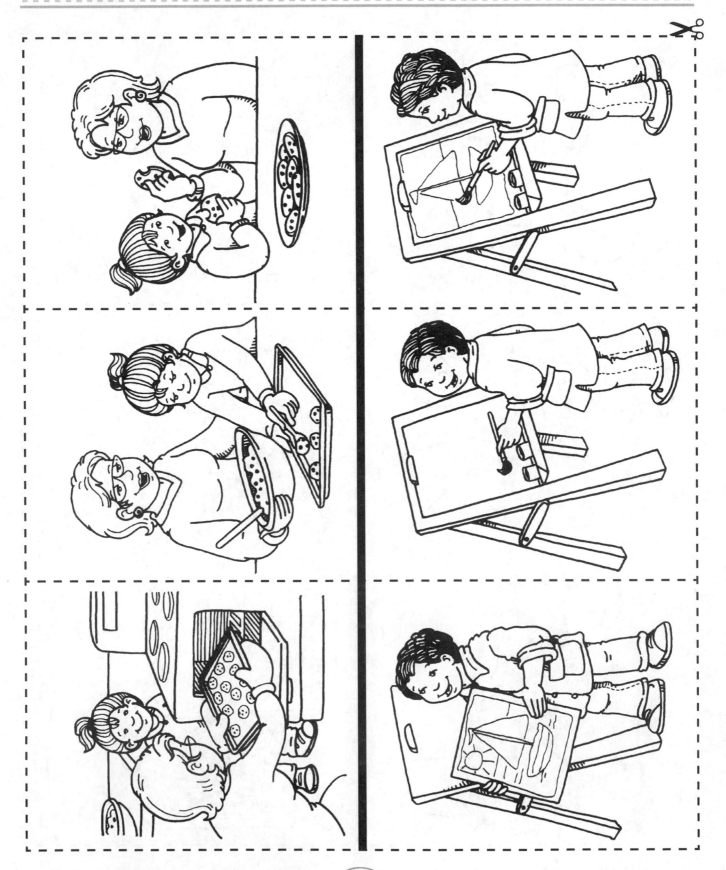

Story Picture Patterns

Draw your own picture.

Draw your own picture.

Draw your own picture.

Making a Time Line

Materials

- *A Busy Year* by Leo Lionni (Alfred Knopf, 1992)
- *The Grouchy Ladybug* by Eric Carle (HarperCollins, 1996)
- full-year calendar poster
- kraft or butcher paper
- large stick
- sentence strips
- watercolor marker

Skill Builders

- conventions of print
- sequencing events
- telling time

Getting Ready

- Draw a large, blank time line on both sides of a long sheet of kraft or butcher paper.

Extending the Lesson

- Help the children map out personal time lines on sentence strips. Encourage them to plan stories that cover a specific time period, such as a day, week, or year. After they have chosen and written about the events, the children may also be interested in creating drawings to explain the events further.

Activity

A time line tells a story that follows a sequential order. A time-line story can cover events of a single day, one year, or even longer. A biography is a good example because it follows a person's life from an early age through adulthood. Introduce this concept to the children by talking about the various activities that happened the previous day.

Read aloud the book *The Grouchy Ladybug*. Ask the children guiding questions about the main character and discuss pertinent vocabulary words. Then reread the story and mark the occurrence of each event on the sheet of kraft paper to fill in the time line. Include a brief description of the event. After writing the descriptions, be sure to reread the words aloud to reinforce the link between spoken language and print.

During another class session, turn over the kraft paper to reveal a second time line. Tell the children that you are going to read a book and would like them to discover the time line. Begin reading the book *A Busy Year*. After the first month is mentioned, stop and see if anyone can guess the time line. Repeat this step each time a new month is mentioned and continue until the children recognize the pattern. Encourage them to guess which month comes next as you continue to read the story. (If appropriate, refer to a calendar poster to help the children see the progression of months.) When you are finished, have the children help you fill in the time line for the book.

Science Connection: Shadow Time Line

Place a large piece of kraft paper on the ground in a sunny spot outdoors. Drive a large stick into the center of the paper. Trace the shadow of the stick and mark the time of day. Write down what the class is currently doing at that time. Have the children predict what will happen to the shadow when you check it in an hour. Continue observing the shadow and marking its placement periodically throughout the school day.

On the next day, discuss the shadow paper, noting any details that were left out. Wrap up the project together by writing a time-line story that incorporates the events that were recorded.

Grab-Bag Stories

Materials

- construction paper
- crayons
- index cards
- paper bags
- pattern page 47
- puppets
- scissors and tape
- small objects or pictures to represent different words
- traditional picture books

Skill Builders

- sequencing events
- recognizing main events of a story

Getting Ready

- Print the simplified text of a familiar traditional story that has been retold in a picture book. (*Note:* Condense the story so it is not too long.) Make four or five copies of the story. Cut apart each copy of the text into five or six sections and store these in a paper bag.
- Make grab bags for the writing center. Write story topics, such as "tiger" and "farm," on index cards. Place each card in a separate paper bag. Also include an object that is a visual representation of the word. For example, place a plastic toy or small picture of a tiger in the bag with the word *tiger*.

Activity

Gather the children in a group. Read aloud the selected picture book and then review the main events of the story. Divide the class into small groups. Tell the children that while you were preparing the stories for them today, you had a scissors accident and the stories were cut into pieces. Explain how you need their help to put the stories back together. Hand each group a paper bag with the story pieces inside. Tell the groups that they are to reassemble the pieces of paper in the correct order. Once they have reordered the story, have them tape the text onto a sheet of construction paper. When they are finished, gather all groups together again. First, talk about the beginning of the story. Then have the children identify the end of the story. Finally, talk about how sometimes the middle section of the story can have many parts to it; however, when all middle parts are together, the story makes sense. Reread the story and have the children check their compilations, making any changes to the text as necessary.

Alternatively, repeat the same preparation steps for other traditional stories that are familiar to the children. Laminate all of the parts. Then place each cut-up story text with its corresponding picture book in a paper bag. Add these materials to your writing center.

Extending the Lesson

Invite each child to write a story about a selected topic, elaborating with description and other details. Prior to the lesson, make copies of the blank sequencing pattern on page 47. Have the children individually choose a prepared bag that contains a story topic. Encourage the children to begin by drawing pictures about the three parts of their stories on the pattern page. Then have them write their descriptions.

Dramatic-Play Connection: Puppet Stories

Young children may enjoy using puppets to reenact familiar stories. Begin by gathering an assortment of puppets for the dramatic-play area. To quickly set up a puppet theater, cover a table with a heavy blanket. Now the puppeteers can perform without being seen.

Catch and Write a Fishy Story

Materials

- chart paper
- donut-shaped magnet
- dowel rods
- heavy card stock
- paint (red, yellow, and blue) and paintbrushes
- paper
- paper clips and string
- pattern page 51
- plastic spoons
- polystyrene foam plates

Skill Builders

- letter recognition
- conventions of print

Getting Ready

- Copy the fish pattern onto heavy card stock and cut out the pieces. Make as many copies as needed.
- Write letters on one set of fish. Make multiple copies of each letter.
- Write common words on a second set of fish. Choose easy-to-read nouns and other high-frequency words, as well as common verbs, such as *run, climb, eat, jump, read, sit,* and *walk.* Also include participles (e.g., *running, climbing, eating,* etc.).
- Secure a paper clip to each fish shape.
- Make fishing poles by tying a length of string to one end of each dowel. Tie a donut-shaped magnet to the loose end of the string.

Activity

Divide the class into small groups. Place the lettered fish on the floor in a big circle. (*Note:* Select letters that are developmentally appropriate for the children to practice identifying.) Determine beforehand how many letters each child will collect. Explain the procedure to the children about "catching" fish from the fishpond and then divide the class into groups. Give each group a fishing pole. Once all of the group members have caught some fish, have them pool their letters into one big pile. Using those letters, direct the children to see how many words they can create, writing them on a sheet of paper. Alternatively, have young children dictate words that begin with the letters displayed on the fish. Record those words on a piece of chart paper.

Extending the Lesson

Challenge beginning readers by providing some fish that have words printed on them. For those children just learning how to read, include drawings of simple objects (noun: fish) and stick figures demonstrating actions (verb: fishing) along with the words. Have each child catch five fish and try to use at least three of the words in a simple "story" that could be just one or two sentences in length. Invite the child to write the story on paper and illustrate it. Younger children who use mock-style writing can easily draw pictures for their stories.

Art Connection: Fishy Colors

Pour red, yellow, and blue paint into individual containers. Write the names of these three colors on a set of fish that you have already cut out. Using the fishing pole, direct each child to catch two fish with different color words. Then have the child place a spoonful of each of those colors on a small foam plate, mix the colors together with a paintbrush, and use the new color to paint a picture. When finished, the child may dictate or write about the picture.

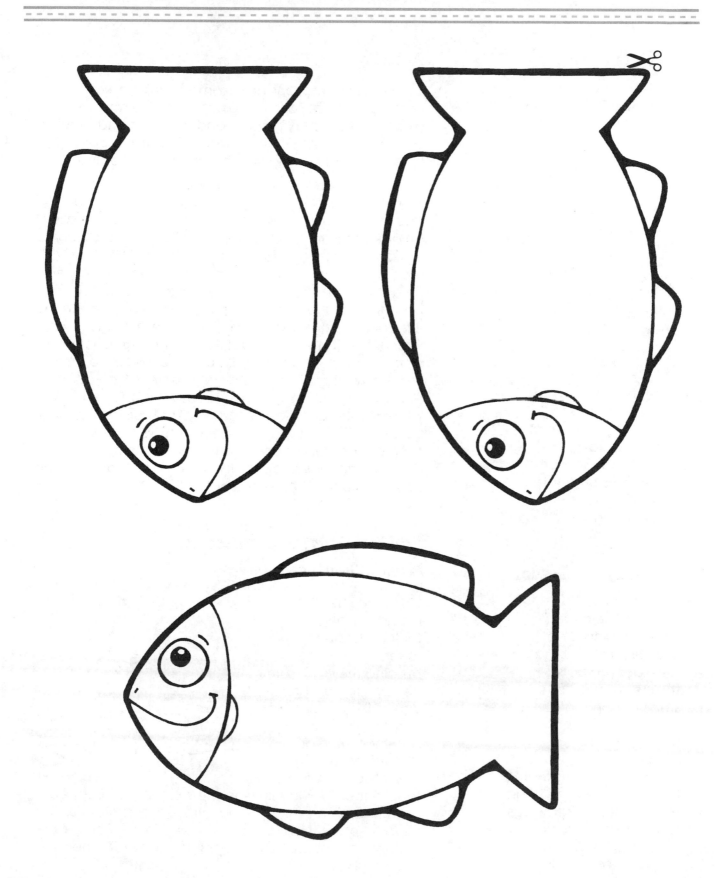

Write and Do

Materials

- bread
- building blocks and tray
- butter knife
- grape jelly
- paper plate
- pattern page 53
- peanut butter
- poster board
- sentence strips
- tape

Skill Builders

- writing instructions
- following directions

Getting Ready

- Write the title "Making a Peanut Butter and Jelly Sandwich" a sheet of poster board.
- Place the sandwich ingredients on a table.
- Make copies of the pattern page for the writing center.

Extending the Lesson

- Have each child select a topic for an instruction sheet. Encourage the children to select projects that require just a few steps to complete. If appropriate, have them fill in copies of the pattern page when composing their instructions. The children may generate drawings for their instructions before compiling the pages into a booklet.

Activity

Written instructions are an important type of communication. For example, they tell us how to assemble toys, play games, and use tools and machines properly. Discuss with the children why it is important when writing instructions to be clear and thorough.

Tell the class that they are going to write an instruction guide on how to make a peanut butter and jelly sandwich. Remind the children that there is an order to writing instructions, just like writing a story. Choose one child to give you the first direction for making the sandwich. Write it down exactly as stated on a sentence strip and tape the paper to the poster board. Continue until the instructions are complete. At this point, do not worry if you know the instructions are wrong or in the wrong order, just record the comments as they come. Follow the directions explicitly to make the sandwich. (Chances are that there will be a few errors in the written instructions, and the children will enjoy the chaos that ensues as you build your sandwich.) After completing the sandwich, ask the children for suggestions about how they would alter the original steps to clarify the directions. Make another sandwich using the revised instructions.

Problem-Solving Connection: Write, Then Build It!

In the block center, provide writing materials for the children to use to record how they are building their structures. Perhaps the children would like to construct very simple structures and then write or dictate instructions so someone else can rebuild them without seeing the examples. Direct each child to use only three or four different materials and have no more than four steps of directions. Set the instructions and building blocks on a tray for others to assemble.

Write-and-Do Form

Name _____   Date _____

Directions: Write your instructions below.

How to _____

Step One: _____

_____

Step Two: _____

_____

Step Three: _____

_____

Step Four: _____

_____

Brainstorming

Materials

- 2 large boxes
- assortment of familiar and unfamiliar items
- construction paper
- fork
- old magazines and catalogs
- paint and string
- paper and pencils

Skill Builders

- abstract thought
- writing as a form of communication

Getting Ready

- Gather two assortments of objects. For the first set, gather familiar things, like a spoon, pencil, block, and so on. For the second set, try to collect objects that are unfamiliar to the children, such as a staple remover, potato masher, etc.
- Place each set of objects in a large, separate box.
- Fold several sheets of paper in half lengthwise.

Extending the Lesson

- Create a "Book of Useful Stuff" by having the children clip pictures of objects from magazines or catalogs and think of new names and descriptions for those objects.

Activity

Sometimes, people use familiar things in unique ways. To begin the discussion, show the children a fork. Ask them to identify the object and describe how it is used. Then talk about how a fork could also be used for making interesting prints with paints.

When we want to write about something new, it is sometimes helpful to "brainstorm." Brainstorming happens when you create a list of ideas about a topic. Just remember that all ideas are acceptable because no answer is wrong. Discuss with the children how they should simply try to think of every possible idea about a subject and write it down—no matter how silly or unreasonable it may seem. This way, many ideas can come pouring out of their heads without restriction.

Choose one item from the box of familiar objects and have the children help you create a list of possible uses for this item. Next, choose an item out of the box of unfamiliar objects and have the children create a list of possible uses for that item. When this list is complete, discuss which list was more difficult to generate: the one where there was already a known use for the object or the one for the unusual object.

Have each child work with a partner and generate ideas about each object in the boxes. Taking turns, one child can be the scribe for the team and write the ideas in one column of the folded piece of paper. Use the other side of the folded paper as well as the back side for more objects and ideas. At the end of the session, gather all of the children together and discuss their brainstorming ideas for a few of the objects.

Art Connection: What Is It?

Make unusual figures with paint and string. Have each child fold a sheet of construction paper in half. Open the paper and spoon a small puddle of paint on the paper close to the fold. Place a piece of string in the fold and carefully refold the paper, leaving one end of the string poking out. While holding the paper closed with one hand, have the child draw the string out of the paper with the other hand. Open the paper again to reveal a painted image. Encourage the children to brainstorm captions for their works of art.

Change-ups

Materials

- baking sheet
- index cards and markers
- paper
- sand, cornmeal, or shaving cream
- sentence strips
- tape and scissors

Skill Builders

- conventions of print
- letter recognition

Getting Ready

- Write word families on separate index cards. Suggestions include -an, -ap, -ar, -eep, -ick, -ig, -ight, -ink, -it, and -op.
- Make several sets of letters and letter clusters on separate index cards, such as b, br, c, d, f, fr, g, gr, h, j, k, l, m, n, p, pr, r, s, sh, sl, st, t, tr, and w.
- Create mini-books for the children to use. See pages 18–20.
- Write simple sentences on paper strips.

Extending the Lesson

- Discuss how the meaning of sentences can be changed by substituting one word. Example: "The girl ran fast." You can change the word girl to dog, ran to ate, or fast to slowly. Have the children revise the simple sentences written on paper strips.

Activity

Talk about how easy it is to alter a word by removing or changing just one letter. Demonstrate this concept by writing the word *stick* on chart paper. Cross out the letters *st* and add the letter *p*. Have a child read the new word *pick*. Continue in the same manner to create other rhyming words.

Divide the class into small groups of three or four children. Give each group a set of letter cards and one of word family cards. Have the groups see how many words they can create by changing the first letter(s) in the word. Direct the children to take turns recording the words. When all of the groups are finished, have the children share their words with the class and then display the papers in the writing center.

Alternatively, provide a mini-book titled "Words I Know" for each child. Have the children practice the same activity by writing different words for one of the word endings in their books. (*Note*: For children in kindergarten, give credit for any word, whether it is a real word or not. Children in first grade should be able to produce actual words.)

Small-Motor Connection: Writing Words

Fill a baking sheet with a shallow layer of sand, cornmeal, or shaving cream foam. Have the children copy words in the textured layer with their fingers. Then have them erase the first letter of each word and substitute it with a different letter to make new words.

Story Webs

Materials

- luncheon-sized paper plates
- pattern page 57
- scissors
- tape or stapler
- watercolor markers
- yarn

Skill Builders

- conventions of writing

Getting Ready

- Cut six 2 ft. (61 cm) lengths of yarn.
- Make copies of the story-web template and place them in the writing center.

Extending the Lesson

- Consider creating a few story-web jumbles by writing a main idea and several supporting details of a familiar traditional story on a sheet of paper. Have the children organize the ideas on the story-web page.
- Have the children develop main character webs using familiar stories, such as "Goldilocks and the Three Bears." Write the name of the character in the center oval and then include descriptive words about the character in the surrounding spaces.

Activity

A story web is a tool that is used to organize ideas. It highlights one main theme and then helps you identify secondary ideas that relate to the main idea. To demonstrate how to use a story web, have the children help you build a graphic organizer using seven paper plates and pieces of yarn. Write the main idea on a paper plate. Tape this plate to a wall or staple it to a bulletin board in the middle of the space. Write supporting details about the main topic on the remaining paper plates. Then tape one end of a piece of yarn to the back of each plate. Attach the other end of each yarn piece to the main-idea paper plate. Finish the display by arranging the supporting details around the main idea. To illustrate, if the story will be about Rover the dog, write *Rover the dog* on the middle plate. Then think of personality traits and actions that could describe the dog, such as *curious*, *digs holes*, *hides his bones*, *rolls in the dirt*, *fetches sticks,* and *likes to be petted*. Write each supporting detail on a separate plate. Now that you have organized your ideas, you can begin to compose the story about Rover, using one concept from your story web at a time.

Encourage the children to build their own story webs, using the pattern page template. Other story-web formats may include the following:

- Person—Write the main idea on the torso, and use the arms, legs, and head for the story parts.
- Popcorn—Present the main idea on the bucket and the story elements on the popped popcorn kernels.
- Flower—The middle of the flower displays the main idea and the petals feature the supporting details.

Math Connection: Math Webs

Create paper plate-and-yarn webs using math concepts. Write a number on a paper plate. Provide additional paper plates and pieces of yarn in the math center. Invite the children to think of creative ways to represent that number and then write that idea on a paper plate. The math web will continue to grow as children think of numerous possibilities.

Making a Story Web

Name _____

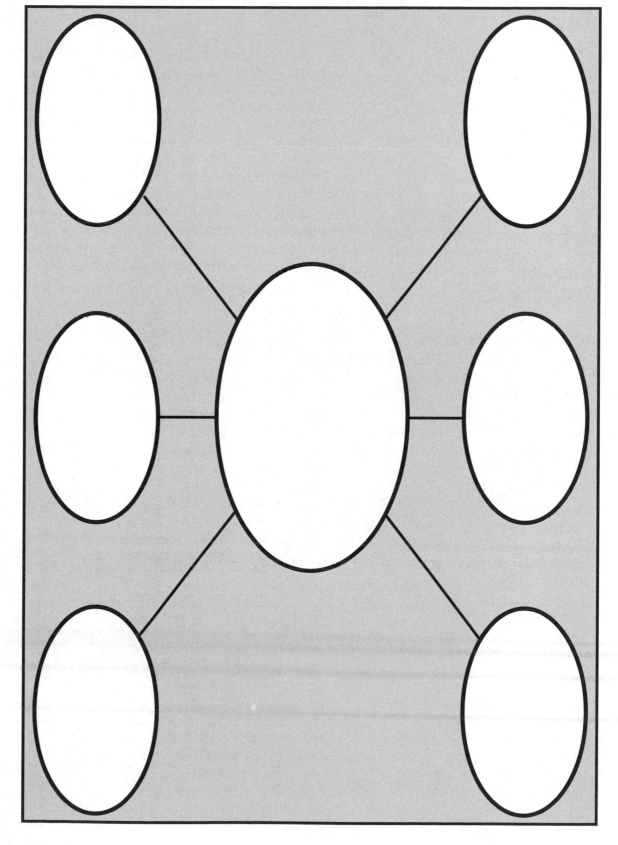

Rhyme Time

Materials

- card stock
- construction paper
- nursery rhymes
- paper and pencils
- poster board
- scissors and tape
- video camera

Skill Builders

- phonological awareness
- conventions of print

Getting Ready

- Print a familiar nursery rhyme on poster board or a white board.
- Create a video set background by hanging a sheet or blanket on a wall.

Extending the Lesson

- Think of different ways to make these sentences rhyme: "I like you better than [add a word]. I like you so much, [add a phrase ending with a word that rhymes]."
- Extend this lesson by having the children create other two-line rhymes (couplets). They can write the rhyming phrases on the inside of handmade greeting cards. (*Note*: Fold sheets of construction paper in half to make the cards.)

Activity

Consider having the children play with rhyming words. Perhaps you can recall times when you overheard children talking about words, obviously enjoying their discovery that those words rhyme. Hopefully, for this activity that joy of discovery will happen again. Have all of the children stand in a circle. Ask the first child to say a word. (This can be any word, including names, places, or silly words.) The next child in the circle should say another word (nonsense or real) that rhymes with the first word given. Continue around the circle until everyone has had a chance to add a rhyming word. Repeat the game, allowing the second child in the circle to start with a new word.

Once everyone has had an opportunity to start a rhyme chain, sit down as a group for a discussion. Ask, "What makes words rhyme?" Choose a favorite nursery rhyme and have the children change it by thinking of a different rhyming word for the end of each phrase. Write the nursery rhyme on poster board or a white board. Have the children choose two rhyming words. Write their rhyming words on card stock. Tape the words on the board to complete the nursery rhyme and then read aloud the revised text. Display that rhyme and other Mother Goose rhymes in the writing center. Provide the necessary materials so that the children can write different rhyming words to change the texts.

Music Connection: Musical Rhymes

Introduce the idea of setting the new Mother Goose rhymes to music. Discuss as a class how to use the new rhyme in a music video. The children will have to compose the music (you may suggest using a familiar tune), rehearse the song, decide how to dramatize the verses, and then videotape their production. When the work is completed, celebrate with a party for the class. Enjoy viewing the children's rhyming antics with popcorn and beverages.

Diamond Poems

Materials

- pattern page 60
- watercolor markers

Skill Builders

- conventions of print
- following directions
- expanding vocabulary

Getting Ready

- Make copies of the diamond poem forms for the children.

Cat
Small, soft
Purring, playing, barking
Loyal, friendly
Dog

Activity

Quite often, people confuse rhymes with poetry. While many poems have stanzas that end with rhyming words, not all do. Poetry is a form of writing that expresses feelings and observations through words and phrases rather than through descriptive paragraphs, or *prose*. One form of poetry that does not contain rhyming words is the *diamante* poem. A diamante poem expresses thoughts about a pair of contrasting subjects by using a series of descriptive words. The diamond poem is a simplified type of the diamante poem. It has five lines that are formatted in the shape of a diamond.

Use the following rules when writing a diamond poem:

- **Line one:** Choose a one word subject that can be contrasted with the subject in line five.
- **Line two:** Write two words to describe the subject.
- **Line three:** Write three words (participles) that end in either *ing* or *ed*. The first word describes the subject in line one. The second word describes both subjects. The third word describes the subject in line five. Alternatively, have all three words describe both subjects.
- **Line four:** Write two words to describe the word on line five.
- **Line five:** Choose a one-word subject that can be contrasted with the subject in line one.

Write a diamond poem as a group or share the provided example to demonstrate how the poem is created. Give each child a copy of the diamond poem form if appropriate. Have the children begin by writing down two subjects that can be contrasted. Record these words on the top and bottom lines. Fill in the rest of the poem by following the rules stated above. Have the children copy their poems onto construction paper and then illustrate them by drawing a picture of one subject at the top of the page and the other subject at the bottom of the page.

Science Connection: Science Poems

Have the children create diamond poems about science concepts, such as spring and fall seasons, rain and snow, heavy and light objects, specific large and small animals, and so on.

 # Diamond Poem Templates

Name _____   Date _____

Name _____   Date _____

Shoelace Stories

Materials

- 2 large boxes or plastic tubs
- art materials
- interview printed in newspaper or magazine
- large sheets of paper
- paper cutter
- pattern page 62
- tape

Getting Ready

- Cut several 1 in. (25 mm) wide strips of paper using a paper cutter.
- Tape several paper strips together end-to-end to create one long strip for each child.
- Make a copy of the Interview Form for each child.

Extending the Lesson

- Let each child choose a famous or imaginary person to "interview" for a story. Have the child answer the questions on the Shoelace Interview Form as he thinks that person would answer the questions. When the form is complete, the child can use those notes to compose a story about the chosen person.

Activity

For this experience, the children are going to be "reporters." A reporter often asks another person questions in order to write a story. Read aloud a short clip from an interview printed in a newspaper or magazine. Then tell the children that they are going to conduct their own "shoelace" interviews and talk to the owners of special shoes. Review the Shoelace Interview Form so that the children understand the questions. Remind them that as reporters they should take notes during the interview and that they will be using those notes to write their reports.

Now the children should be ready to interview their classmates. First, have the children individually take off one of their shoes. Divide the class into two groups. Have Team A place their shoes in the first container. Team B will drop their shoes in the second container.

Give each child an Interview Form. Ask every member of Team A to select a shoe from the second container, find the shoe's owner from the other team, and then interview that person. Give the children a few minutes to complete their interviews and take notes. At the appropriate time, have the teams switch roles. Give Team B an opportunity to conduct the interviews. Have each of those children choose a shoe from the first box and interview its owner.

Finally, give each child a long strip of paper. Tell the children that these paper strips are "shoelaces." Using the information from their interviews, the reporters write their stories on the paper shoelaces. When everyone is finished, gather the children and have them share their reports with the class.

Art Connection: Interview Portraits

A report would not be complete without a picture. This time, have your young reporters become portrait artists or make collages to highlight special interests. They can use art materials and collage supplies to create their art. Direct each reporter to incorporate at least one detail from the interview into the portrait. Mount each piece of art alongside the final copy of the shoelace story.

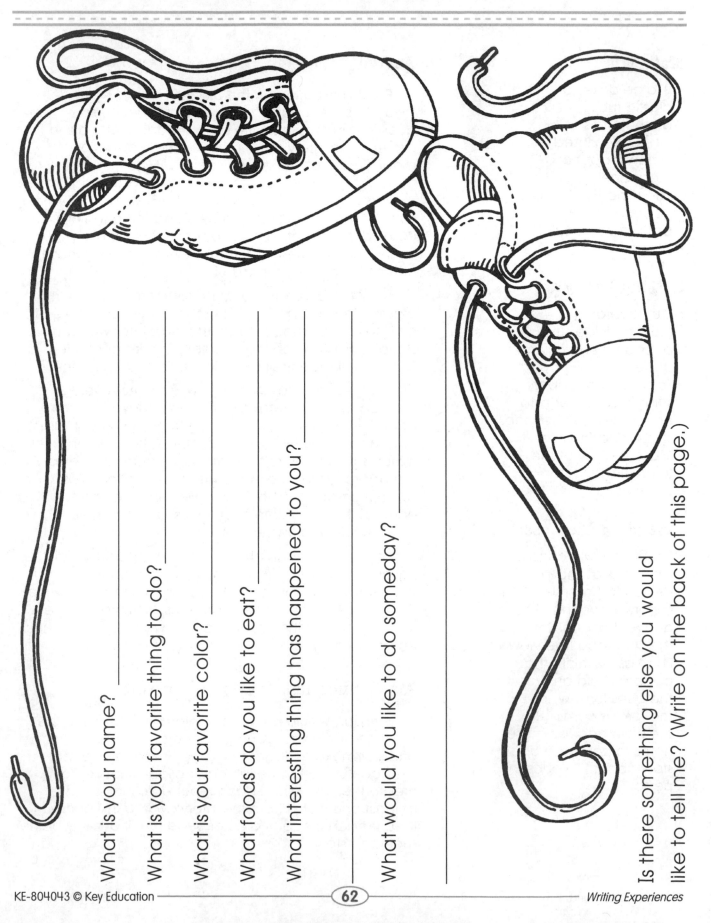

What is your name? _____

What is your favorite thing to do? _____

What is your favorite color? _____

What foods do you like to eat? _____

What interesting thing has happened to you? _____

What would you like to do someday? _____

Is there something else you would like to tell me? (Write on the back of this page.)

Journaling

Materials

- jar or other container
- paper
- pattern page 64
- scissors
- stapler

Skill Builders

- creative exploration
- writing as a form of communication

Getting Ready

- Assemble a mini-book for each child. (See the directions on pages 18–20 for various book forms.) Alternatively, staple several sheets of paper together to make a "notebook" that can be stored in a folder.
- Make a copy of the Journaling Prompts and cut apart the topics into strips. If possible, think of other topics that may interest the children in your classroom and write those ideas on slips of paper, too. Store the journaling prompts in a container.

Extending the Lesson

- Encourage the children to choose entries from their journals that can be developed into more complex writing pieces. Have each child revise the writing and add illustrations.

Activity

Journaling is one instructional tool that encourages writing every day. A mini-book or folder filled with paper can be used by each child for recording personal thoughts, observations, daily experiences, and so on. The topics can be as broad or as narrow as you please, and can be teacher or child generated. However, most importantly, the topics must be meaningful to the children as writers.

Journaling Tips

- Keep the journals easy to access since the children will be using them frequently.
- Date each entry. This way, if pages get removed or placed out of order, they can be put back in the correct sequence quickly. Having a date on each page will also be helpful to see the progress the children are making as they perfect their writing skills over time.
- Let the children use their journals as opportunities for freewriting experiences. You may wish to use samples from entries to individualize instruction in the areas of handwriting, spelling, or punctuation, but the bulk of the journal work should simply be for writing enjoyment. Young children can dictate or use invented spellings when recording ideas in their journals.
- Generate a variety of topics so that the novelty of writing will engage young writers every day. Alternate "free-choice topic" days with days when specific topics (e.g., My Trip to the Zoo) or open-ended statements (e.g., My favorite animal is . . .) are used.
- Store the journaling prompts in a jar, hat, shoe, or other container. (Containers can also be representative of thematic units or special holidays, such as a pumpkin for Halloween.) Allow one child to choose the journal topic each day.
- Be sure the journal topics and prompts are relevant and interesting. If children refuse to write about certain topics, give them the opportunity to generate their own ideas to stimulate creativity with words.

 # Journaling Prompts

- My favorite thing to do with my family is . . .
- The thing I like to do with my friends most is . . .
- I was the most scared when . . .
- Things I like to do with my dad . . .
- Things I like to do with my mom . . .
- Things I have learned since I was a baby . . .
- If I were planning a party, I would plan to . . .
- The first time I lost a tooth . . .
- My first day of school . . .
- I am happiest when . . .
- Last weekend I . . .
- Someday I will invent . . .
- If I had a million dollars, I would . . .
- When I grow up, I will . . .
- My favorite place to visit is . . .
- I was the bravest when . . .
- My pet . . .
- My favorite holiday . . .
- If I were the parent and my parents were the kids . . .
- Things I like to do at night . . .
- My best friend . . .
- When I am all by myself, I like to . . .